MW01124618

Copyright Notice

Strolling Around Toledo by Irene Reid

ISBN: 9781520222196

All rights reserved. This book may not be reproduced in any form, in whole or in part, without written permission from the author.

The author has made every effort to ensure the accuracy of the information in this book at the time of going to press, and cannot accept responsibility for any consequences arising from the use of the book.

Potted History

Toledo is a very old city. It sits on top of a granite outcrop in the middle of Spain, and there are many legends about its origin – invented over the centuries by the various races that lived there. Some say Hercules built it, others say it was built by Brutus of Rome, and there is the tale that it was built by the Jews who fled from the destruction reigning down on Jerusalem from King Nebuchadnezzar of Babylon.

People have certainly lived there since the Bronze Age, but the first people we know about were the Jews who arrived in 500 BC and named their city Ṭulayṭulah – so perhaps they were indeed escaping from King Nebuchadnezzar.

Toledo gets its first mention in the history books by the great Roman historian Livey, who renamed the city Toletum and described it as:

> Parva urbs, sed loco munitia
>
> Small city but well-fortified

Toletum was swept up into the Roman Empire and was soon promoted to a Municipium which meant that the town's citizens became Romans – a great privilege. Along with that promotion came all sorts of Roman goodies - public baths, a circus for chariot races, an amphitheatre, and vitally a city wall.

As everyone knows, Rome fell when the Barbarians from the North marched south. The Visigoths were a Christian tribe from what is now Germany, who moved southwest and into Spain. They liked Toletum so much they made it their capital. However the Visigoths were not the greatest builders in the world, so although they were rulers for a couple of centuries, there is not that much evidence of their reign – some have affectionately called them The Invisigoths.

The Visigoths were in turn ousted from power by the Moors who crossed over from North Africa. The Moors took over much of Iberia including Toletum, which by then was called Toledo. The Moors stayed as rulers for several centuries, and unlike the Visigoths they did build and decorate their cities.

So for a time Toledo was home to Christians, Muslims, and Jews. You will read a lot about how the three religious groups lived in harmony, but religious intolerance always gained the upper hand. The Christians marched down from the North and after many years and battles the Moors were pushed out of Spain and back to Africa. Toledo then became the favourite city of the royal family and the centre of Spain's Catholic Church.

Toledo's Jews suffered attacks twice in the fourteenth century greatly reducing the population. Further restrictions, laws, and discrimination, later made life so difficult that many of the survivors converted to Christianity or gave up and left, virtually wiping out Toledo's Jewish population

Toledo however thrived as the capital of Spain and the head of the Spanish Catholic church. The city was then dealt a fatal blow by King Philip II when he decided to move his court to nearby Madrid. Toledo lost influence, people, and money - while Madrid did exactly the opposite. Toledo managed to hold on to its religious power for a long time, but eventually even that was taken by Madrid. Toledo went into hibernation and has survived very much intact because it was mostly forgotten about.

It did flicker into life again during the Spanish Civil War and the Siege of the Alcazar, but once peace returned Toledo slumbered again. Nowadays its old town is a draw to tourists and lovers of history and art – even if the locals prefer to move out to the modern suburbs.

El Greco

Toledo is a treasure house of El Greco masterpieces, and he is the reason many tourists visit. El Greco came from a wealthy family from the Island of Crete. He studied art and travelled to

Italy. He tried to make his fortune in Rome but made the mistake of criticising Michelangelo:

A good man, but he did not know how to paint

He was more or less shunned by Rome so he sailed to Spain and finally found success in Toledo where he made his home. His real name was Doménikos Theotokópoulos which was clearly too difficult for the Spanish, so he became El Greco, The Greek. As you explore you will find many of his wonderful paintings, in churches, museums, and even hospitals.

Once you have seen one or two, you will find it very easy to recognise his very distinctive style – his paintings are very colourful with strangely elongated figures and an otherworldly feeling.

Tourist Bracelet

Visitors to Toledo can buy the Tourist Bracelet. At the time of writing, it only costs 9 Euros and gives you unlimited access to seven sights for as long as your bracelet remains intact. The sights included are:

- Colegio de Doncellas Nobles
- The Jesuit Church
- San Juan de los Reyes
- Cristo de la Luz
- Santo Tome
- Inglesia El Salvador
- Santa Maria La Blanca

They are all interesting to have a look around and are included in the walks, so the bracelet is worth buying if you intend to visit everything. You can buy it any of the included locations.

The Walks

There are 2 walks. If you are only in Toledo for the day you should follow Walk 1 which will take you to the most famous sights including the Cathedral and the Juderia – The Jewish Quarter.

If you have more than one day, Walk 2 will take you to some lesser known places including some Roman sites, a walk through a series of old city gates, and a visit to see some of El Greco's work, both inside and outside the old city walls.

The Maps

There are maps sprinkled all through the walks to help you find your way. If you need to check where you are at any point during a walk, always flip back to find the map you need.

Walk 1 – The Highlights

This walk starts in Toledo's largest square Plaza Zocodover.

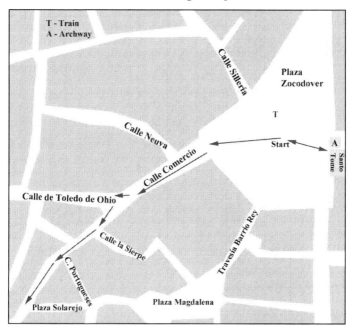

Plaza Zocodover

This is Toledo's busiest square. The square is ancient – it was originally used by the Romans and its name is from the Arabic Suk-aldawad which means Market of the Beasts. Later it hosted bullfights, fairs, and of course the trials of the dreaded Spanish Inquisition. Now it's full of restaurants, bars, and shops.

If you have time later, you could buy a ticket from the kiosk on this square, and catch the little tourist train – it will take you outside the city and up to the opposite hill where you will get a great view of the Toledo skyline and its wall. However there is a lot to see in Toledo before you do that.

Orientate yourself by spotting the only archway on the square. The original archway was built by the Moors and was at that time the only entrance through the old city wall.

It's called the Arco de la Sangre which translates as the Arch of Blood. If you look above the archway you will see a narrow chapel topped by a clock. The chapel contains a statue of "Christ of the Blood" – hence the name given to the archway. The chapel is not open to the public, but at Easter the custodians fling open the windows and if you happened to be standing on Plaza Zocodover that day, you would be able to see the statue through the large central window. The original statue belonged to the "Brothers of the Blood", and it was their job to pray for the unfortunates who were condemned to death. They helped and guided them spiritually from the moment of sentencing to the final execution.

Another macabre story from the history of Plaza Zocodover involves the "Brotherhood of Charity". If a body was found in Toledo or perhaps pulled out of the Tagus, and if no obvious family could be located, the body was placed in a large enclosure on the square. The brothers would then encourage the citizens to donate to give the dead a decent burial. Just imagine that sight on a hot Spanish day!!

To the right of the archway you will see the Santo Tome confectionary shop.

Marzipan
Toledo is famous for its marzipan, and it claims that the nuns of the Convent of San Clemente in Toledo were the first to come up with the recipe. During the battles between the Moorish Kingdom in the South and the Christian armies of the North, famine stalked the land. Almond trees grew like weeds around the cities of Castile and oddly there was no shortage of sugar. So the nuns made a paste of sugar and almonds and used it to feed the starving.

Once peace settled marzipan was firmly established as a favourite confection, so the nuns kept making it. Today you can buy marzipan products from shops all over Toledo, and even from some of the convents. You might be tempted by the marzipan delights in front of you but you should hold off buying until you return at the end of the walk. You might even find other inviting confectioners as you explore.

Stand with your back to the archway and walk straight ahead to the other side of the square. When you get there turn left to leave the square by Calle Comercio – old Toledo's main street.

Ohio
You can peruse the shop windows as you walk downhill towards the Cathedral – you can see the Cathedral tower peeping above the rooftops. Pass Calle Neuva on your right. The next street on your right is Calle de Toledo de Ohio – it slopes upwards away from Calle Comercio.

Of course Toledo has been twinned with its namesake in Ohio since 1931and named this street to commemorate the event. The street-sign makes a nice snap - the circle on the top left holds the Great Seal of the State of Ohio.

Continue downhill passing Calle de la Sierpe, Cuesta de la Portugueses, and Plaza Solarejo on your left.

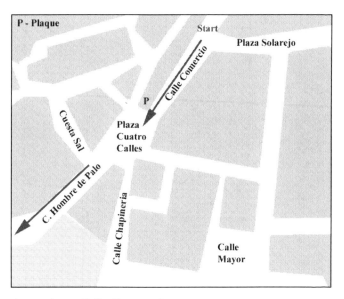

Continue along Calle Comercio.

Plaza Cuatro Calles

When the street opens out into little Plaza Cuatro Calles you have reached the commercial heart of old Toledo – called the Alcana. This is where the five main shopping streets from long ago converged, each little shop run and owned by Toledo's Jewish merchants. There is a plaque on your right as you enter the square; it commemorates the fact that Cervantes mentioned the Alcana in Don Quixote, Chapter 9:

> "One day, as I was in the Alcana of Toledo, a boy came up to sell some pamphlets and old papers to a silk mercer"

You will see two possible exists ahead of you. The left hand road, Calle Chapinería, goes downhill towards the back of the Cathedral, but you should take the right hand road, Calle Hombre de Palo.

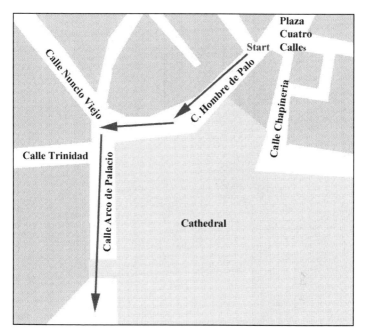

You will soon find the Cathedral wall on your left and behind it is the Cathedral Cloister. It was added in the fourteenth century; built on top of an old Jewish market area which had burned down in a convenient fire just as the Cathedral needed space to expand. Follow the wall around into Calle Arco de Palacio.

Calle Arco de Palacio

This street runs between the Bishop's palace on your right and the Cathedral on your left. You can see a bridge linking the two buildings, presumably so the Archbishop didn't have to mingle with ordinary people when popping in for a mass. It's actually a seventeenth century replacement for the original fifteenth century bridge which caught fire and was destroyed. Continue into Plaza del Ayuntamiento and to the front of the Cathedral.

Plaza del Ayuntamiento

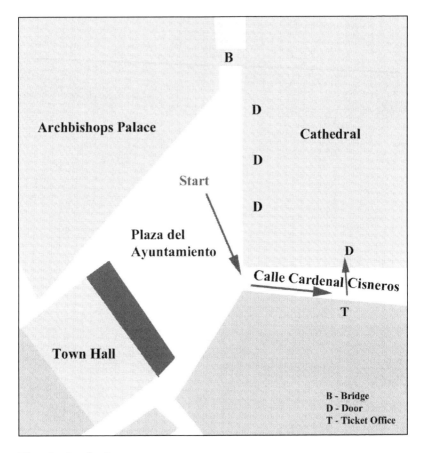

The Cathedral

As you gaze up at this huge edifice, you have to agree that Toledo's cathedral is one of the most magnificent in Spain – and much more interesting than the usurper Madrid's rather modern cathedral, which was only completed last century when Madrid finally seized the archbishopric from Toledo. This is in fact Spain's second biggest church, only beaten by Seville.

The Cathedral sits on an ancient site which has always been used for religious purposes. The Visigoths built a church there all the way back in the 6th century. That church survived for a time after the Moors invaded, but eventually it was destroyed and replaced by a Mosque. Of course when the Christians again regained control of Toledo it was only a matter of time before the Mosque was turned into a church. That church lasted until the thirteenth century. The Pope then gave the nod for a cathedral, so the old church was demolished and this cathedral was begun.

You can see that there is a bell tower on the left, but instead of a second tower on the right there is a dome. They did plan a second matching tower but discovered that the foundations weren't up to it due to a stream which runs under the cathedral. So the Cathedral has a lopsided appearance.

If you were to climb the Cathedral Tower you would have to tackle 284 steps and you would meet the Campana Gorda (the fat bell) which weighs in at 17 tons. It is reputed to be the largest bell in Christendom and legend says that when it rang out for the first time, it shattered all Toledo's windows. It's also said it took four hours to haul Campana Gorda up and hang in the tower. These days it is no longer rung as it has a fracture, so you would hear a clank rather than a bong. At the time of writing the tower is closed to visitors.

The Cathedral has three main doors. The door in the middle is The Door of Forgiveness, on the right is The Door of Final Judgement, and on the left is The Door of Hell. It's said that you are forgiven your sins if you enter through the Door of Forgiveness. Interestingly there is no mention of what happens if you enter by the Door of Hell or the Door of Final Judgement! But of course you won't get the chance to find out as you can't enter by any of those doors. Cathedrals always insist on visitors entering by a side door, and their grand doors are only opened on very special occasions.

It's not surprising really that this Cathedral was chosen when a dramatic ecclesiastical backdrop was needed in the film The Three Musketeers. Cardinal Richelieu is carried across Plaza

13

Ayuntamiento with the Cathedral providing an imposing backdrop.

Before moving on, take a look at the two lines of statues above the main door – they are very mobile and almost look as though they are dancing.

The Town Hall

Facing the Cathedral, turn right to find the lovely town hall which stands behind a little rectangular pool of water. You can find the Tourist Information office on the ground floor – handy for any maps or reservations you might need.

The Town Hall is classed as a Renaissance building, which basically means it is symmetrical and follows the Greek and Roman style of building – lines of columns are typical.

Archbishop's Palace

Face the Town hall and the very large Archbishops Palace is on your right – it's the one with two statues above the door. Way back in the thirteenth century, King Alfonso VIII gave a couple of houses next to the cathedral to the Archbishop to use as a residence. With each new Archbishop, the building got bigger and grander, presumably to reflect the importance of Toledo.

Above the door stand four nymphs and between them and the balcony you can see two columns. They are all that are left of the original shield which used to stand where the balcony is now. The columns represent the Pillars of Hercules, which according to the myth stood in the Strait of Gibraltar. They were emblazoned with "Non Plus Ultra" which means "No Further", as that was the end of the known world to the Greeks. Spain of course had ventured much further and crossed the mighty Atlantic Ocean, so King Carlos I added the pillars to his shield but changed the words to "Plus Ultra" meaning "Further".

The ticket office for the Cathedral is actually around the corner, so face the Cathedral once more and follow it round to the right into Calle Cardenal Cisneros.

Calle Cardenal Cisneros

You will find the Cathedral ticket office not too far along on your right, opposite the Cathedral entrance. You can only buy your ticket in that shop, not in the Cathedral itself. The tickets are not cheap but you do get a lot for your money. You can explore the huge Cathedral, its extensive museum, and you even get an audio guide to help you understand what you are seeing – and it's all worth a visit.

Inside the Cathedral

Inside you can see a forest of 88 columns, flying buttresses, rib vaulting, and pointed arches. Stand at the end of one of the naves and just gaze down it at the column of arches marching before you – you might have to imagine the other tourists away.

Use your audio guide which will take you to the main sights in the Cathedral. It will take you around the Cathedral first, then through a maze of little rooms and corridors where you can see the Cathedral's treasures, out to the cloister, and finally returning you near the same door you started at. Here are some favourite items to spot as you explore.

Red Hats

As you explore look up to see if you see any red hats suspended from the ceiling. If you do it belongs to a Cardinal who has passed away - his hat is hung in the cathedral until his body has decomposed. It does make you wonder how they check!

Saint Christopher

You don't see paintings much bigger than this one. It's ironic that one of the largest paintings in the Cathedral is of a saint who the Catholic Church has demoted. In the sixties he was removed from the official list of saints, as the church decided he had never really existed.

Capilla Mayor

The huge golden altarpiece tells the story of Christ. It's enormous - it reaches to the ceiling and is full of intricate detail - it starts with the nativity at the bottom and ends with the crucifixion at Calvary at the top.

El Transparente

One of the highlights of the Cathedral is El Transparente, which you will find behind the altar; it's made from marble, jasper, and bronze. For many years it was ignored because the sculpture was in a gloomy corner of the Cathedral and not appreciated. Later a hole was cut through the wall of the Cathedral to let shafts of sunlight hit it. Another hole was cut at the back of the altar so that worshippers could see through the altarpiece into the tabernacle. The sculptors then used angels, saints, and prophets to hide the holes and to reflect the sunlight back and forth to wonderful effect. If you are lucky to visit on a bright day you will see the result.

Ochavo

The Ochavo is a lovely octagonal chapel designed by El Greco's son Jorge Manuel Theotocopoulos – he also painted the frescoes high above you. The chapel was closed for a long time due to neglect but has since been restored to its full glory

Choir

The two-tier choir in the centre of the Cathedral is very beautiful. The walnut seats are all decorated. Most interesting are the lower seats which are decorated with scenes of Moorish cities surrendering to the Christians. The upper seats show biblical scenes.

Just in front of the choir is a wonderful statue of a delighted Mary with her son. I love the way Jesus is touching his mother's face.

Behind this lovely statue you will see the blue glow of the Rose Window – the oldest in the Cathedral with 750 pieces of stained glass.

Capilla Santiago

Saint James was beheaded by King Herod, and according to tradition his body was taken to Santiago de Compostela in Spain, so he is honoured in churches all over Spain. Here you can see the Saint slaying the Moors.

The two marble tombs you can see are Álvaro de Luna and his wife. He was a self-made man who rose in Spanish politics and became the Grand Master of the military order of Santiago – which is why he lies here and is flanked by the Knights of Saint James. Alvaro made a very wise career move by befriending the young and weak King John II, and became his advisor and protector - at least until the king married savvy Isabella of Portugal, who set about getting rid of Luna as soon as she could. She convinced the king that he should be executed, so Luna was given a cursory trial, condemned, and beheaded in 1453.

The Sacristy

When you walk in you will be awed by the ceiling – a glowing heavenly scene. Once you stop looking up, you will find that this is a room for the art lovers. It's home to paintings by El Greco, Caravaggio, Van Dyke, Titian, Goya, and others

As you explore Toledo you will hear about King Wamba who was considered the best of the Visigothic Kings. His remains have moved about a bit. He was first dug up by Alfonzo X who put them in Santa Leocadia church which you will visit later. While the King was at it, he also moved the remains of Wamba's father, King Recesvinto. They were both moved again in 1845, put into coffins lined with red velvet, and placed in the Cathedral. They are both now in the Sacristy.

El Espolio – El Greco

This was one of El Greco's first works and he ran into trouble with the Inquisition because of it. His crime was placing Christ below the onlookers, and believe it or not he was tossed into prison because of it. However he had already made vital friendships within the church and was released.

The painting shows the moment when Jesus was disrobed before the crucifixion, and while Jesus looks to heaven, his seething accusers point fingers and argue over who is going to get the red robe. At the bottom we see a man drilling a hole into the cross in readiness for the crucifixion while Mary looks on.

Twelve Apostles - El Greco

Think of it as a bible cast list as you peruse along the line of paintings. El Greco did two groups of the apostles, and this one is not complete, but you can see a complete set if you visit the El Greco Museum later on this walk.

Cloister

The cathedral has a lovely two tier cloister covered in murals and you can walk along one side of it. You can't actually walk into the cloister garden but you should be able to spot the well.

On August 15th the church holds a Day of the Assumption festival. It's a little different from most church festivals because glasses of water from the cloister well are given to all visitors. This dates from the seventeenth century when worshippers at the festival were fainting from the heat and leaving in droves. So the Cathedral authorities decided to distribute water to cool the worshippers down, and a tradition was born. Visitors can even fill up bottles of the waters from the well to take home. So if you visit on that day, make sure you have a sip.

The cloister also contains an inscription which commemorates its Visigothic origins:

> En el nombre del Señor fue consagrada la Iglesia de Santa María en católico,
>
> el día primero de los idus de abril,
>
> en el año felizmente primero del reinado de nuestro gloriosísimo rey Flavio Recaredo,
>
> Era 625 [13 de abril de 587]

It translates as;

> In the name of the Lord the Church of Saint Mary was consecrated as Catholic,
>
> the first day of the ides of April,

> in the joyful first year of the reign of our most
> glorious king Flavius Reccared,
> Era 625 [13 of April of 587].

If it's open, climb up to the second floor of the cloister and find the 20 foot statues which are carried in procession on holy days.

San Blas

From the cloister you can reach San Blas, another kaleidoscope of colour which was originally a burial chamber. If you take the time to look at the murals you can see the Life of Jesus, with depictions of the Annunciation, the Nativity, the Crucifixion, the Ascension, the Final Judgment, and the Resurrection.

Monstrance

This huge golden object sits in the middle of the treasury - it's called a monstrance and is where a priest will place a piece of the Eucharist for the faithful to worship. This one is made of solid silver gilded with gold which it is said was brought back to Spain by Columbus. The monstrance is taken out to join the holy procession during Corpus Christi.

Descension Chapel

This chapel is thought to be where the altar of the original Visigoth church stood in the 6th century. There is a legend that the Virgin Mary appeared in this chapel to speak to Saint Ildefonso – you will read more about him later on in the walk. The stone the Virgin stood on is in an iron protective casing, and there is a mosaic tile next to it which says

When the queen of the heavens put her feet on the ground

She put them on this stone

Kiss it for your consolation

Touch the stone saying with total devotion

"Revere this place on which the Holy Virgin put her feet"

You can discreetly slip your hand through the grill to touch the stone if you like.

Mozarabic Chapel

The Visigoths are not completely forgotten – if you visit at nine in the morning for mass you can hear the Mozarabic Rite in the Mozarabic Chapel. When Toledo was reconquered by the Christians there was a dispute over which mass should be used in Toledo, the Latin rite which is used in the rest of Europe or the Mozarabic rite which is what the Visigoths used before the Moorish invasion

To decide, both books were put into a fire by Cardinal Cisneros. The Mozarabic Rite survived in much better condition than the Latin Rite, perhaps because it was written on thick heavy vellum whereas the Latin Rite was on thin paper. Anyway God had spoken, so in Toledo they still use the Mozarabic Rite – the only place in Europe still to do so. Pope Gregory VII did try to get rid of it but failed, and when Pope John Paul II visited, he used both in his masses.

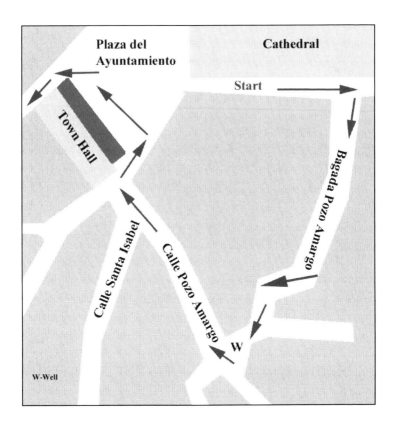

When you exit the Cathedral turn left and take the first right into Bajada Pozo Amargo. This narrow street will wiggle left and right and take you downhill and into a little square where your will find an old well.

Fernando and Raquel

LEYENDAS TOLEDANAS

"EL POZO AMARGO"

Las lágrimas que el recuerdo, añoranza del amado causaron en una joven toledana, amargaron las aguas de este pozo.

Tertulia Zocodover

E.T.R.T.
2001

Don Fernando was a Catholic lord who fell in love with Raquel, the daughter of Levi the Jew. He would slip out of his home at night when all of Toledo was asleep and make his way through the narrow streets which you will be exploring soon. When he reached Levi's home, Raquel would be waiting for him on her balcony. Fernando climbed the ivy over the wall and waited by this well for Raquel, and when she arrived they would

23

hold hands in the moonlight, and talk long into the night while sitting on the rim of the well.

One night Fernando was ambushed and run through with a sword while he waited by the well. Levi had hired an assassin to kill him to save his daughter's reputation. Raquel was grief-stricken and every night she would sit by the well and weep. One night she looked into the well and saw Fernando looking up at her, so Raquel reached down to him and fell into the well to her death.

Find the little plaque which says:

> "The tears of longing for a beloved caused a young Toledana to salt the waters of this well'.

You will read a lot about "Toledo, The City of Three Cultures" as you explore. It's certainly true that the Christians, Jews, and Muslims did tolerate each other in Toledo to some degree, but the story of Ferdinand and Raquel tells us that there was a limit to that tolerance.

Leave the little square by Calle Pozo Amargo, which is on the far right hand-side side of the square as you entered it. It will take you back uphill, and at the top turn right to return to Plaza del Ayuntamiento. Stand facing the town hall and then go round its right hand side.

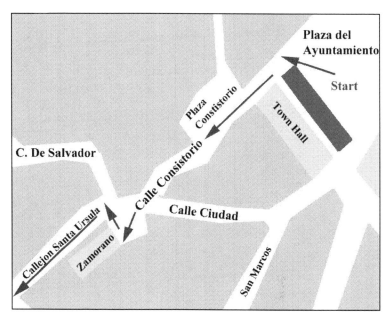

This will take you up some steps and into a lovely little square, Plaza Consistorio. Walk across this square to enter a covered little street called Calle Consistorio. You will see a plaque at its entrance which tells you that the Mayor used to live above the passageway. Go through the passage and you will reach another little square where you will find the shop of Mariano Zamorano in the diagonally opposite corner.

Swords

If you have ever watched a movie with El Cid or Zorro swashbuckling around, they were probably wielding a Toledo sword.

Toledo was the centre of the world for sword making, and the reason they were so successful was that they learned how to temper steel – and they kept it a closely guarded secret. Sword making ran in families and each family only passed their secrets onto their sons.

The crucial point in sword making is how long the blade stays in the furnace. The timing used by each master sword maker was never written down, but memorised in song. As a sword was being forged the master would hum the tune and use the rhythm to time his work. Toledo swords were the strongest but still light and easily manoeuvrable. Anyone who was anyone invested in a sword from Toledo. Each sword had to be tested to make sure it made the grade, and then it was marked with the workshop's logo.

Sword makers in other countries tried to emulate Toledo swords but no-one managed to do it. Of course swords are not in such demand these days, but some ceremonial swords are still made for the military. Mariano Zamorano is one of the most traditional sword-makers, still making his blades on the premises.

If you feel the urge to own a sword, pop in to have a look. The gleaming blades you see hanging on the wall are either factory made, or if they have an artisan label, they were made in the shop – the artisan blades cost more but are very striking. Even if a sword is not really your thing there are many other tempting items.

With the shop door behind you, turn left and left again to leave the square via narrow Callejon Santa Ursula. The building on your right as you walk along Callejon Santa Ursula is the Convent of Santa Ursula.

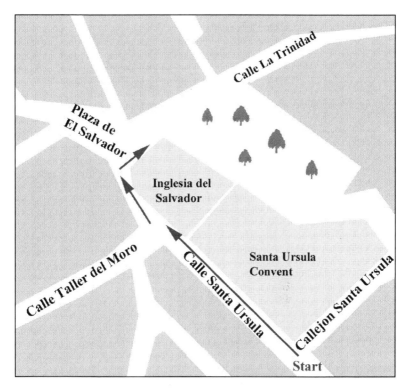

When you reach the T junction with Calle Santa Ursula, turn right and follow the convent wall.

Convent of Santa Ursula

The Convent of Santa Ursula is one of the oldest convents in Spain – it was started in 1260.

Saint Ursula's story is a bit fanciful. She decided to travel from Britain to Rome in the company of 11,000 virgin handmaidens. This was at a time when the choice was either walk or ride a horse, so already the logistics are incredible. They had the bad luck to run into a tribe of Huns in Germany, and Ursula was given the choice of marrying the chieftain or dying along with the eleven thousand virgins. She refused to marry and they were all slaughtered. It seems an odd qualification for sainthood.

Continue along Calle Santa Ursula and when you reach Plaza El Salvador you will find the church of San Salvador on your right.

Iglesia San Salvador (Tourist Bracelet)

Pop in to have a look around this ancient building.

Once inside descend some steps to explore the archaeological dig and see the oldest remains. You will reach an open area which has a mixture of Roman, Visigothic, and Moorish ruins. The large horseshoe arches are Moorish, but they are built on top of Roman and Visigoth columns. You can climb the spiral stairway to a gallery which gives you a better view of the carvings on the columns. If you pop a Euro in the box at the far end of the gallery, it will switch on some lights to let you see the carvings more clearly – I had to hit the box on the side to kick it into action!

Back upstairs, you will see a line of roman columns and at the end a Visigoth pilaster – a pilaster is a decorative rectangular column. You might be able to identify some biblical scenes on this one, such as the Resurrection of Lazarus, but notice that most of the faces have been scraped off – because of course Islam forbids images. Their removal proves that the Visigoth church was converted into a Mosque when the Moors arrived. Above the columns is yet another line of Moorish arches running the length of the church. The bell tower is built on top of the original minaret.

Finally you have today's church. Legend tells us that Queen Berenguela of Castile was travelling through Toledo when a tremendous storm started and her party was forced to seek shelter in the Mosque. They prayed to God and the storm stopped, so Berenquela had a word with her husband, King Alfonso VII, and the Mosque was converted into the San Salvador church.

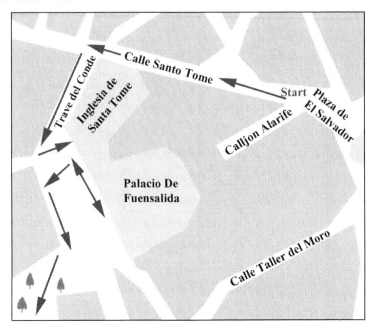

Cross the square in front of the church to leave by Calle Santa Tome. Pass Callejon Alarife on your left, and then take the next left, narrow Travesía del Conde which runs along the side of the Iglesia de Santo Tome.

You will pass a door on your left in Travesía del Conde which you can use to visit the church itself if you wish – most tourists just press on to reach one of Toledo's highlights which is just a bit further on.

Santo Tome (Tourist Bracelet)

When you reach the end of Travesía del Conde you will find another entrance to the Santo Tome church on your left. It is used to let tourists in to view El Greco's masterpiece, The burial of the Count of Orgaz. There is usually a queue but it moves reasonably quickly.

It's a beautiful painting. At the top you see heaven and below earth. It tells the story and legend of Don Gonzalo Ruiz who came from Toledo and who was a very pious man. Orgaz also gave large amounts of money to this church which happened to be El Greco's parish church.

The church should also have received more money from the town of Orgaz. At least that is what the Count intended but it seems that the town ignored the will for 200 years. A priest then took the council to court and won his case, and El Greco was commissioned to paint this masterpiece to commemorate the event.

Legend tells us that when the Count died, Saint Stephen and Saint Augustine arrived from heaven to bury him with their own hands. You can see the two saints in their golden robes, busy at work while the mourners look on. The Count is being lowered directly into his grave and not into a coffin, so it's a nice touch that the Count's tomb is below the painting.

The mourners are actually a Who's Who of the time the painting was produced, although we can only identify a few of them. The robed chap on the far right is the priest who commissioned the painting. El Greco is in the middle looking back at you – he is just above the Saint's upraised hand. Finally the little boy is El Greco's son, and if you look at his handkerchief you can see it has El Greco's name on it

Palacio de Fuensalida

Just next door to Iglesia Santo Tome is the Palacio de Fuensalida – a Moorish palace which is now the central office of the President of Castile.

It was home to Isabella of Portugal who was the wife of the Holy Roman Emperor Charles V. She lived there while The Alcazar was being refitted for the royal family. However poor Isabella also died here in childbirth. She and her husband actually loved one another, quite an unusual thing in Royal circles, and her death so young affected him deeply. He never married again and dressed in black for the rest of his life.

At the time of writing you are able enter the ancient doorway with its columns and lions, climb the monumental staircase, and visit the beautiful courtyard. There are moves to provide guided tours of the palace so perhaps when you visit they will be available.

Make your way back to the Iglesia Santo Tome and then face away from the door. There are five steps in front of you which will take you down into Paseo Tránsito where you turn left.

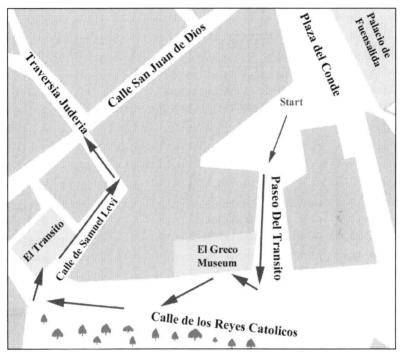

Follow this little road as it slopes downhill, veers a little to the right, and finally takes you to the El Greco Museum. Just outside the museum you will see a memorial to Amuel Halevi

Amuel Halevi

Amuel Halevi is better known as Samuel Levi, who was an important character in the story of the Jews in Toledo. He started with nothing, but managed to work his way up to be chamberlain and finally treasurer in the court of Pedro I. He became exceedingly wealthy and built the Synagogue of El Tránsito which you will see shortly.

His luck ran out when the King turned against the Jews and accused Levi of stealing. Levi was imprisoned and tortured to try to get him to reveal where the treasure he was said to have stolen was buried – but Levi refused to speak and died under torture. To this day, people still wonder if there is a great fortune buried somewhere in Toledo.

El Greco Museum

This museum complex stands near where El Greco's house once stood. It was thought that one of the old buildings in the museum grounds was in fact his house, however it's since been discovered that El Greco's house was destroyed in a fire and the house in the museum belonged to Samuel Levi. If you go in to the museum you can also visit the house. You might be surprised to see the floor-mats which everyone used to sit on the floor – as was the custom in Spain in the 16th Century.

There is also a modern extension and inside there is a little cinema where you can watch an informative film about El Greco – try to see that before you explore the rest of the museum.

There are some interesting paintings to have a look at.

If you visited the Cathedral's Museum you may have seen the series of paintings of the twelve apostles by El Greco. The museum also has a series so you can compare the two, but the general opinion is that this is the better version.

Here are some favourites to hunt for:

The Tears of Saint Peter – El Greco

El Greco has painted Saint Peter weeping because he had taken fright and disowned Jesus when he was arrested. If you

34

look carefully you can see that the Saint's eyes are filled with tears. He is also carrying his famous keys.

In the background you can see Mary Magdalene running to find Saint Peter having just been told by an angel about Christ's return.

San Bernardino of Siena – El Greco
This epitomizes El Greco's way of painting elongated figures and pale faces. At his feet you can see the three mites which represent Siena, Ferrara and Urbino. Bernardino was asked to be Bishop of all three but declined.

San Juan Evangelista – El Greco
This shows us the story of Saint John being tested by a priest at the Temple of Diana in Ephesus. The priest challenged John's God by giving him a cup of poison and declaring that if his God was real the poison would not harm him. God responded by

turning the poison into a dragon which flew away, letting Saint John drink safely from the cup.

View and map of the town of Toledo – El Greco
The young man holding the map is thought to be El Greco's son. See how many of the sights you can spot.

When you exit the museum turn right along Paseo Tránsito which will merge into Calle de los Reyes Catolicos. Continue along Calle de los Reyes Catolicos - You are now in the Judería, what was once a thriving Jewish community. You will come to the Sinagoga El Transito on your right.

Synagogue of El Tránsito
Toledo was home to one of the most prosperous Jewish communities in Europe until the Black Death arrived in the fourteenth century. As happened all over Europe, the frightened Christians blamed the Jews for the disaster and attacked and murdered Jewish homes and families.

King Pedro tried to make amends for the anti-Jewish riots. He gave permission to the Jewish Treasurer Samuel Levi to build a new synagogue. Levi was very wealthy and planned a beautiful building – he even imported cedars from Lebanon in honour of King Solomon who built the first Temple in Jerusalem.

However good relations between the Catholic Church and the Jews didn't last – all Jews were expelled from Spain in the fifteenth century by Catherine and Ferdinand, the Catholic Monarchs. The Jewish community tried to persuade the King and Queen that the Toledo Jews had arrived in Spain before the crucifixion and had nothing to do with it. All to no avail – it's estimated that over half a million Jews refused to convert to Christianity and had to leave Spain or face execution – religious tolerance was at an end.

Since then the synagogue was used by various Christian bodies before becoming a military barracks. In the 18th century it was dedicated to the Tránsito de Nuestra Señora (meaning Mary's assumption into heaven), which explains its odd name. It's now restored and is a museum where you can wander among the remnants of the Jewish culture in Spain. In fact there are only three medieval synagogues left in Spain, two in Toledo and one in Cordoba.

The prayer hall, the Gran Sala de Oración, has been restored so you can enjoy the wonderful Mudejar decoration and its wonderful pine ceiling. The walls are covered with Hebrew and Arabic inscriptions, as well as delicate geometric and floral shapes.

When you leave the Synagogue turn left along Calle Samuel Levi - named after the treasurer you just read about.

As you explore this area you will see some colourful plaques on the walls commemorating Toledo's legends and famous citizens. This one is titled "The Treasure of Samuel Levi".

Follow this little street as it turns left and takes you to a crossroads.

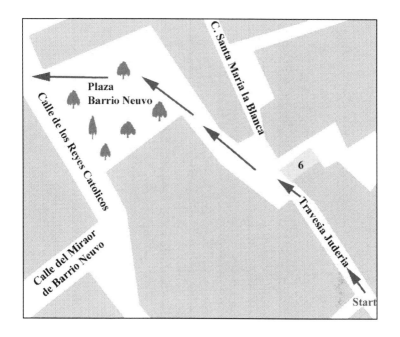

Cross over into Travesía Judería and at number 6 on your right you will find The Jewish House.

The Jewish House

You are now in the heart of Jewish Toledo and this house dates back to the fourteenth century. Legend says it once belonged to Ishaq Abravanel, a Jewish moneylender who financed the voyage of Columbus which discovered America.

If it's open you can visit and see the basement where there are purification baths which would have been used in preparation for religious events. As you descend you will pass through a doorway and on it there is an inscription which is from verse 21 of Psalm 118:

I thank thee, that thou hast answered me

Once back outside, continue in the same direction and you will reach a fork in the road. Take the left hand road into tree-filled Plaza Barrio Nuevo. This used to be the Jewish market place and is perhaps a nice place for a refreshment.

Leave the square diagonally opposite the corner you entered it by.

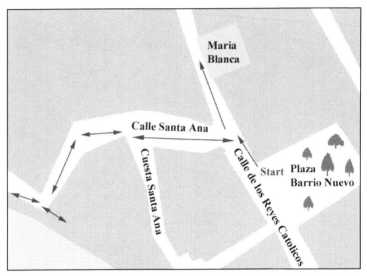

Turn right to continue along Calle de los Reyes Catolicos but only a few yards and then turn left into Calle Santa Ana. Follow this street and it will take you down to a view point.

Roca Tarpeya

As you face the river the Roca Tarpeya is on your left – and just behind you on the wall is a plaque which records the legend.

The Roca Tarpeya cliff was named after the infamous Tarpian Rock in Rome, which is where Rome dispatched criminals by hurling them to their death. When the Romans were in power in Iberia, Governor Daciano issued an edict to imprison all Christians and burn their churches and bibles. Any Christian who did not then renounce Christianity was tossed over the Roca Tarpeya to plummet to his death.

Puente de San Martín

Again facing the river, you will see the Puente de San Martin on your right. This lovely bridge with its five pointed arches and defensive towers dates from the 14th century. It bridges the Tagus giving access to the west of Spain. There is a nice legend about its construction.

It seems the engineer got his calculations wrong and realised after the bridge was almost complete, that the central arch was not going to be strong enough to bear the weight of the heavy stones being brought in to build the Cathedral. The Engineer did not know what to do and confided in his wife.

His wife sneaked out during a storm and set fire to the scaffolding holding up the archway, which of course then collapsed. It was assumed lightning had caused the fire and the engineer was called in to repair the damage – and of course this time he made sure that the archway was extremely strong, and built one of the largest and highest arches of the day.

If you were able to see the keystone of the bridge you could decide if it is really the head of Archbishop Tenerio who paid for the bridge, or as the locals claim, the engineer's wife.

Backtrack uphill to Calle de los Reyes Catolicos and turn left. You will find the Sinagoga de Santa María La Blanca on your right.

Sinagoga de Santa María La Blanca (Tourist Bracelet)

This is a much older Synagogue than the Transito you just visited. It was built in 1203 by Moorish craftsmen who were the best in their field. It is a symbol of the time when the three religions of Toledo did actually live in harmony- a synagogue built by Muslim craftsmen under Christian rule.

It survived until the 15th century when it was turned into a church. Since then it went steadily gone downhill as a workshop, a barracks and finally a refuge for ex-prostitutes. However it was saved and restored. In 1992 the King apologized to the Jewish people and ordered that the building revert to being a synagogue – although that is still to happen since there is no real Jewish population left in Toledo.

You can enjoy walking across the red tiled floor through the forest of white horseshoe arches, each decorated in Mudejar style. The lovely columns are decorated with pretty pine cones.

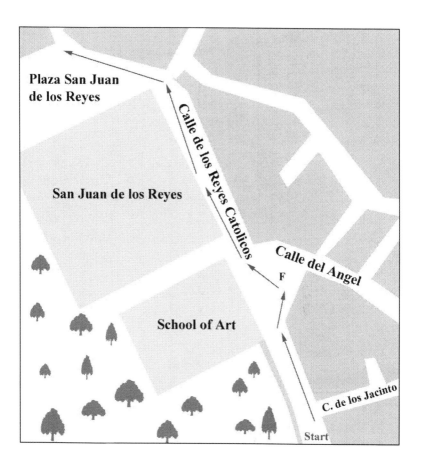

Leave the Synagogue and once again turn right along Calle de los Reyes Catolicos. You will see the handsome School of Art on your left.

School of Art

The school was built under the reign of Alfonso XII in 1881, and was later extended by knocking down the adjacent convent of Santa Ana. It has been dedicated to art education since 1902. Unfortunately it is not open to visitors, which is a shame.

Arquillo del Judío

Opposite the School of Art you will see a triangular plaza with a fountain. Climb up the wide steps behind the fountain and you will see a picturesque little archway which is called the Arquillo del Judío, the small arch of the Jew. The Juderia was kept quite separate from the rest of Toledo and this was one of the doorways which were locked at night.

The Juderia was a city within a city and covered about 10% of old Toledo. As the centuries passed, the fortunes of the Jewish population swung from the good times to the bad times, depending on who was in power and their attitude to the Jews.

There were many attacks over the centuries, but despite this the Jewish population of Toledo grew and gained influence and power. The fabled "living in harmony" mostly occurred in the twelfth century – despite the anti-Jewish laws issued by the Vatican in 1215, e.g. Jews had to wear special clothing to mark them out – does that sound familiar?

The Christians became more and more aggressive to non-Christians. The Jews had to stay behind the walls of the Juderia at night, and could not leave during Christian festivities. Finally the purge began, and the Jews had to leave or convert.

Just next door to the School of Art is the Monastery of San Juan de los Reyes.

Monastery of San Juan de los Reyes (Tourist Bracelet)

The Catholic Monarchs, i.e. husband and wife King Ferdinand II of Aragon and Queen Isabella I of Castile, founded this monastery to celebrate their victory at the Battle of Toro against the Portuguese. However it should be mentioned that the Portuguese celebrated their victory at the same battle, because the outcome was a bit of a draw.

Toledo was chosen to host the new monastery because of its ancient Visigothic role as the capital. It sits in the middle of

Spain and seemed to unite the two kingdoms of Castile and Aragon which is what Isabella and Ferdinand wanted.

Isabella and Ferdinand never missed an opportunity to promote their faith and its supremacy, which is why this imposing Catholic edifice sits so near the old Jewish quarter.

Isabella and Ferdinand also planned to be buried in the monastery. However they later had a change of heart when they finally defeated the last Moorish kingdom of Granada in Southern Spain and named it as their burial site instead.

Inside the Monastery

From the door, you first enter the beautiful two tier cloister with its garden full of orange trees and roses. Walk around to see the ancient carvings lining the walls.

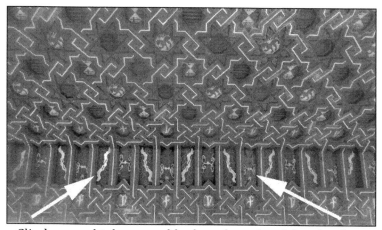

Climb up and take a good look at the colourful red ceiling on the upper level – at its base is a line of Arrows and Yokes, as well as the letter Y and the letter F.

Isabella and Ferdinand made sure they were remembered at the monastery, and you will find The Yoke and The Arrows in various places. Ysabel is symbolised by the yoke, as the Spanish word for yoke is yugo which starts with Y, the first letter of her

45

name. Whereas Ferdinand is symbolised by arrows, as the Spanish word for Arrows is Flecha, the first letter of his name.

Find the doorway into the church – above it you will see an ornate depiction of Saint Veronica holding the cloth she gave Jesus to wipe his head as he carried the cross to Calvary. When he gave it back to her his image was on the cloth. Interestingly one of the manoeuvres made by bullfighters with their capes is called a Veronica – as the cape is held in the same manner as Saint Veronica is usually portrayed holding her cloth.

Once inside the church you can't miss the enormous eagles holding up the coat of arms of Isabella and Ferdinand, and beneath them you can see once again, the Yoke and the Arrows

Napoleon's troops badly damaged the monastery when they occupied Toledo, not only did the church catch fire, the surviving treasures were pillaged by the troops and no doubt carted back to Paris. The resident Franciscan monks were thrown out. Restoration started in 1883 and lasted almost a century – it wasn't until 1954 that the monks could return.

Exit, and with the door behind you, turn left to go around the side of the monastery and into Plaza San Juan de los Reyes. Look up to your left and you will see chains hanging on the outside wall of the monastery. They are from the Christian prisoners freed during the Granada campaign when the Moors were finally defeated and all of Spain was under the rule of Isabella and Ferdinand. The chains were hoisted onto the wall in 1495.

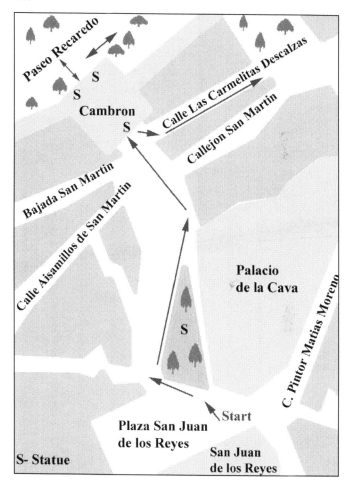

With the Monastery and its chains behind you, leave Plaza San Juan de los Reyes and follow the main road downhill past the beautiful Palacio de la Cava on your right. A statue of a young Queen Isabella stands in front of it.

Palacio de la Cava

There is a legend about the name of the palace – and it has nothing to do with Spain's famous sparkling wine!

Count Don Julian was a Visigoth nobleman and Governor of Ceuta in North Africa. The Count sent his beautiful daughter Floridna to court in Toledo for education and to befriend the Royal Family. One day Floridna was bathing in the Tagus near where you are now, and was spotted by the King. Now the story takes two paths.

The Moorish version tells us the King first tried to seduce her, and when he was refused he raped her.

The Christian version tells us Floridna seduced the King and became his mistress. Floridna became known as La Cava, which means scarlet woman.

Either way she got pregnant. Her father took his revenge by making a pact with the Moorish kingdom in North Africa, aiding them in the Moorish invasion which of course led to the end of the Visigoth Kingdom in Spain. Spain became a Moorish Kingdom. It is said that Floridna haunted the riverside for many years until she was finally exorcised.

Continue downhill and you will eventually reach the Puerta del Cambrón.

Puerta del Cambron

The four-towered gate is named after the cambroneras, or spiny buckthorn bushes which used to grow all around here. It was also historically known as "The gate of the Jews" since it gave access directly to the Juderia. It was originally built by King Wamba – what a great name! He was king of the Visigoths

48

from 672 to 680 and generally regarded as the best king the Visigoths produced.

On this side of the gate you can see Santa Leocadia – one of Toledo's patron saints. She was tortured by order of the Roman Governor but still refused to recant, so she was thrown into a cell and left to die. One night her jailers saw a glow coming from her cell but they were too frightened to investigate. Next morning they found Leocadia lying dead so her body was removed and dumped near the Tagus. Other devout Christians secretly gave her a burial and a cult grew up around her grave. Her remains were dug up and given to a Count from Hainault in Flanders, who had fought in the re-conquest of Spain. He placed her in an abbey in present day Belgium. In the sixteenth century a Jesuit priest retrieved her remains and finally returned them to Toledo in 1587. You will see the Santa Leocadia church later in the walk.

Walk through the gate to see the other side – it has two Visigoth Kings wielding huge swords, Sisenand and Sisebut, guarding the entrance to the city.

Legend says that this was the gate used by Dona Maria Pacheco when she fled Toledo and escaped to Portugal. Her husband had been the commander of the Comuneros in Toledo. Toledo and other towns in Castile rebelled against the government in the sixteenth century, and for a few exciting months the Comuneros held their ground. Maria Paceco's husband was killed in the battle of Villalar, and on hearing the news Maria took command of the city and led the defense until Toledo finally surrendered peacefully six months later – minus Dona Maria Pacheco who escaped to Portugal. She is buried in Porto in Portugal.

In peace time the gate was a tollgate and anyone who was coming into town on business had to enter this way. Even today it is the only gate which traffic actually goes through rather than around.

With the gate behind you turn right to stroll along at the bottom of the old city wall – as this is one of the best sections. However don't go too far along as it's a long walk to the next gate. Instead when you have seen enough, return to the Puerta del Cambron and re-enter the city. Turn left along Calle Las Carmelitas Descalzas.

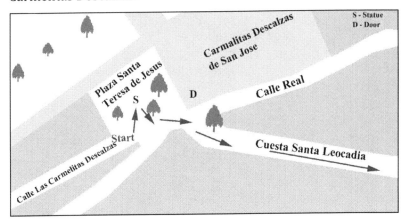

You will soon reach Plaza Santa Teresa de Jesús on your left. There are some trees and benches here if you need a rest.

Plaza Santa Teresa de Jesús

The very modern statue in the middle is Santa Teresa de Jesus herself, better known as Saint Teresa of Ávila. She founded the Barefoot Nuns, who dedicate their lives to prayer, abstinence, poverty, and contemplation. Santa Teresa has been portrayed by some of the world's greatest artists and sculptors, such as Bernini and Rubens.

The building on the right is the convent. Unlike many convents, the nuns have virtually no contact with the outside world – so you won't be buying any marzipan here.

Return to the road and turn left. Just past the convent door you will see two roads leading uphill and a tree between them. Make sure you go up Cuesta Santa Leocadia, to the right of the

50

tree – it has a rather incongruous modern building on the right hand side.

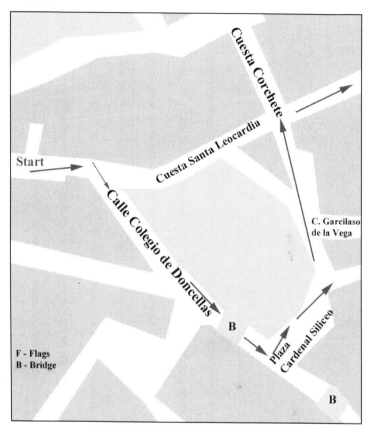

Once you pass the modern building you will see a narrow stepped lane on your right called Calle Colegio De Doncellas. Climb up and when you reach the top, walk straight ahead to go under the pretty bridge linking the buildings on your left and right. The bridge was built to give access from the Colegio de Concellas Nobles on your left to the adjacent building when it expanded. Once past the bridge, turn left into Plaza Cardenal

Siliceo and the building on your left is the Colegio de Doncellas Nobles

Colegio de Doncellas Nobles (Tourist Bracelet)

This is the School for Noble Maidens and you can explore its church.

The school was founded in the sixteenth century and took in pre-teen girls. When the girls left, a dowry was provided for them, or they could always avoid marriage and enter a convent. The only criterion applied was that the girls had to be from "old Christian" families - and that excluded any converted Jewish or Muslim families. The church proposed girls from poor families and the Monarch proposed girls from noble families.

The grand tomb in the centre of the church is that of Cardinal Siliceo who founded the college. If you look at the engravings on the tomb you can see the girls being admitted. It still has a connection to education as the building is now a University residence for female students.

The church used to house two El Greco's which were snaffled by the Cathedral, but there are talks of their return – so you might see them in their original home.

When you exit turn left and when you reach the end of the College turn left to go down Cuesta Corchete. Pass Calle Garcilaso de la Vega on your right and then take the next right which is another flight of steps up to Santa Leocadia church.

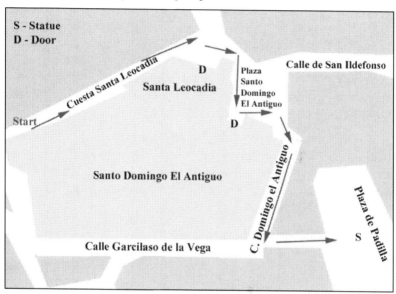

Santa Leocadia Church

According to folklore, the church stands where the saint's home stood. It's a very old church, with parts of it from the thirteenth century. As you reach the top of the steps you can admire the Mudejar facade with its lovely horseshoe shaped door and Moorish decoration over the door. Once around the corner you are in Plaza Santo Domingo El Antiguo.

Walk into the square to see the lovely rounded apse of the Santa Leocadia Church. The door to the Santo Domingo El Antiguo monastery is just beyond it.

Monastery of Santo Domingo

This medieval monastery holds not only some of El Greco's earliest paintings but El Greco himself. The monastery is said to be the oldest in Toledo.

The altarpiece holds The Assumption of the Virgin which put El Greco on the road to success. He got the commission when the very wealthy but pious Maria de Silva died and left a fortune to be used in decorating the convent. El Greco was asked to paint the altarpiece of the chapel in which Maria de Silva was placed. When El Greco's painting was shown it caused a sensation – his colourful and unique painting was quite unlike anything else in Spain. El Greco was a hit! The other paintings on the altarpiece are St John the Evangelist and St John the Baptist on either side, and The Resurrection at the top.

On the opposite side of the church from the door you entered by, you will find a little window which lets you look down into the crypt and what is said to be El Greco's wooden coffin. There are other rooms which you can visit, which are probably of less interest but worth a quick look.

By the way, the nuns of this convent make little biscuits and sweets which you can buy from the nun at the door – worth trying.

When you leave Santo Domingo turn right to continue to follow the Monastery wall into Calle Santo Domingo el Antiguo. When you reach a T junction with Calle Garcilaso de la Vega turn left to climb the steps up to Plaza de Padilla.

Plaza de Padilla

This square is named after Juan de Padilla, one of the leaders of the Comuneros who revolted against King Charles V in the sixteenth century. His statue is in the centre of the square.

The Royal Family in Spain was in a very precarious position, because the crown was held by Charles V who was just six years old, and his mother was Joanna the Mad – not the best choice as a regent. Charles was sent to the Netherlands, and when he returned to claim his crown at sixteen, he didn't speak Castilian and was followed by a retinue of Flemish nobles who expected to rule the country.

The locals were very unhappy with this setup and preferred Joanna the Mad. They called themselves the Comuneros, formed a rebel army, and managed to take control of Castile for over a year. The army was finally defeated in battle and the three leaders, including Padilla, were beheaded. What was left of the peasant army fled and only Toledo held on. Toledo eventually surrendered in 1521

Toledo now commemorates its role as a rebel city, and April 23rd is Castile and Leon day.

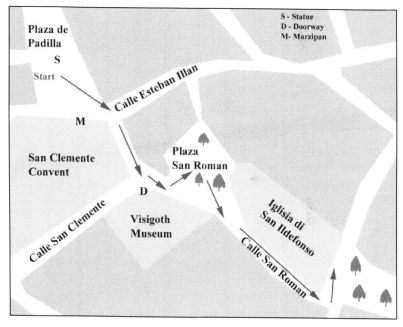

With the stairs you just climbed behind you, cross the square diagonally right. As you do you might find the door to the San

Clemente shop open, and if so you can think about buying some marzipan. Legend tells us it was the nuns of San Clemente Convent who invented marzipan.

Leave by Calle Esteban Illán, but just a few steps later turn right into narrow Calle San Roman. As you climb this little alley you will see another striking horseshoe shaped door ahead of you. It is a part of Iglisia San Roman. It has been deconsecrated and is now the home of the Visigoth Museum.

Visigoth Museum

This museum is where you will find the best of the Visigoth remains in Toledo. As mentioned in the potted history, they are affectionately known as the Invisigoths because they really didn't leave much of a mark compared to the Romans before them and the Moors after them.

You can explore the lovely old medieval church which was built on top of an old Mosque – and you can admire the lovely Eastern style arches and stucco work, with wonderful murals showing various royal character and Biblical scenes. Some people might find the museum actually more interesting than the exhibits.

In the nineteenth century someone dug up the Treasure of Guarrazar – a treasure trove of Visigothic gold and jewelry. The theory is that as the Moors were marching towards Toledo, the treasure was gathered up, taken to the countryside, and buried. It certainly kept it safe as it wasn't discovered until over a thousand years later!

The treasure was displayed proudly in Madrid and Paris. Unfortunately some of it was stolen and never recovered. Also the very best piece, a wonderful golden crown, is now on display in Madrid. It's not clear on what grounds Madrid is holding on to it, and personally I think Toledo should campaign for its return. Regardless, what is left is well worth a look.

Once back outside stand with the door behind you and turn right to follow the museum wall into a lovely area of greenery, Plaza San Roman – it's a good place for a breather. On the other side of the little garden is the Iglesia de San Ildefonso, but you have to follow the church wall all the way along Calle San Roman to reach the front door in Plaza del Padre Juan de Mariana.

Iglisia di San Ildefonso (Tourist Bracelet)

This is a huge church fronted by some mighty Corinthian columns and two flanking towers.

Ildefonso was part of a prominent Visigothic family from Toledo. He was very religious so he defied his family's career plans and instead became a monk. He did very well and eventually became bishop of Toledo.

One day he was leading a mass when the church was filled with light as the Virgin Mary appeared. She gave Ildefonso a sumptuous Bishop's robe as thanks for his work in the church. If you visited the Cathedral earlier on the walk you might have seen the Descension Chapel where this all took place. It was that miracle that caused The Pope to promote Toledo to be the head of the Catholic Church in Spain.

If you go inside the church you will find a bright, airy, and cheerful interior as its walls are brilliantly white.

You should climb the tower where you will get a good view of The Alcazar on Toledo's skyline.

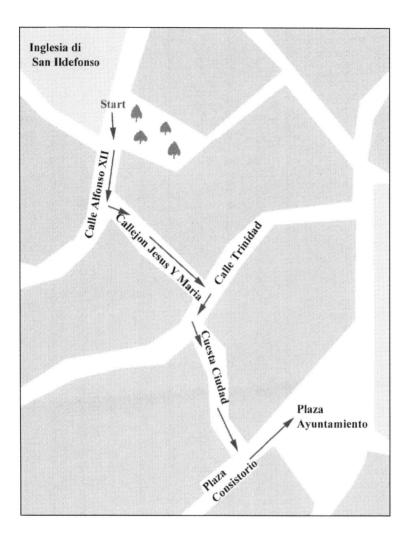

Leave the church and turn right into Calle Alfonso XII, and then take the first left into narrow Callejon Jesus y Maria. It will take you to a T junction with Calle Trinidad. Turn right along Calle Trinidad but take the first left into Cuesta Ciudad.

You will reach little Plaza Consistorio which you might recognise as you passed through it right at the start of this walk.

Turn left to get back to Plaza Ayuntamiento and you have reached the end of Walk 1.

Walk 2 – Gates and El Greco

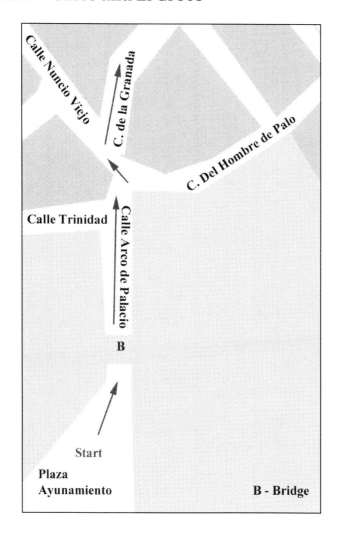

Walk 2 starts in Plaza Ayuntamiento.

Face the Cathedral and turn left to leave by Calle Arco de Palacio. Walk under the bishop's bridge and pass Calle Trinidad on your left. Just after passing Calle Trinidad you will reach a fork in the road. Go left into Calle Nuncio Viejo, but just a few yards and then take the first right into Calle de la Granada.

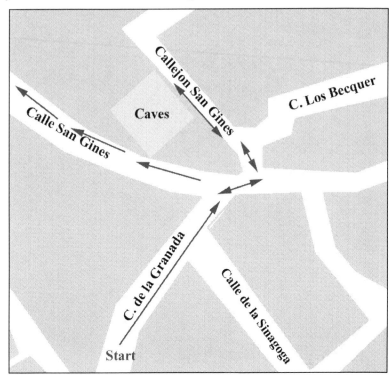

This narrow little street will take you uphill, passing Calle de la Sinagoga on your right as you near the top. You will reach tiny Plaza de San Ginés which is so small it hardly merits the title Plaza.

Leave by turning right but just for a few yards, and then take the first left into another tiny little street. At the end of this little street, ignore Calle Los Bécquer on the right and instead go left into Callejón San Ginés. You will find the Caves of Hercules about one block uphill.

Cueva de Hercules

It's free – so do pop in and climb down the stairs into the Caves of Hercules which sit beneath the site of St Ginés Church. The church was demolished in the eighteenth century.

Legend tells us that the demi-god Hercules founded Toledo and built a sumptuous palace in jade and marble where the church once stood. Beneath the palace in a deep cave, he hid the secret of a terrible disaster which would befall Toledo. He ordered that every King of Spain should add a new lock to the door to the cave and never enter.

Of course that was never going to work. When there were 24 locks on the door, the last Visigoth King, Don Rodrigo, decided to explore instead of adding another lock, all in the hope of finding a great treasure. The Legend tells us that he descended deep into the cave and found a white cloth. When he unwrapped it he saw that the cloth was covered in figures of soldiers, all dressed in outlandish fashion. As he watched, the figures became animated and marched across the cloth. At the bottom of the cloth Rodrigo read

When this cloth is opened, this army will conquer Spain and rule

Rodrigo put everything back and returned to the surface, no doubt crossing his fingers as he did. However as foretold, in 711 the Moors crossed from Africa and overran Spain ending the rule of the Visigoths.

Myths and Legends of the cave multiplied over the years, so in the sixteenth century the church ordered the army to descend into the caves and investigate. They returned to the surface covered in bruises and telling of terrible sights. The Cardinal took the hint and had the entrance sealed.

It was opened to the public in 2010. What you will find is not nearly as exciting as the legend hints at. In fact the experts have decided that the "cave" is part of the Roman water storage system. The site is not very big but there are plans afoot to excavate more – and it's nice to read about the Legend as you have a look around.

When you exit the Caves turn right. Ignore Calle Bécquer which leads away to your left, and instead turn right into the little street you used earlier. At its end turn right again, and you will pass through tiny Plaza de San Ginés again. Keep right to go into Calle San Ginés.

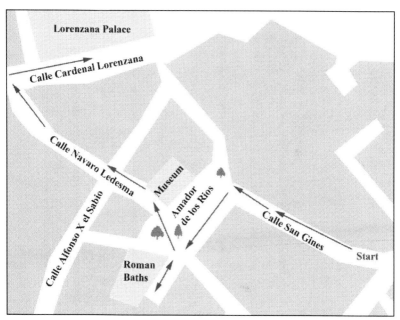

You will come into a nice little square, Plaza Amador de los Ríos, which has some trees and a fountain. Keep left to walk down the left hand side of the square and you will see a little alley in front of you. Go along it to reach the Roman Baths.

Roman Baths

The baths are not huge, but they are free and worth a look. They were only discovered in the 1990's, and the experts have declared that Toledo's Baths were actually built using the latest technology of the time.

Roman Baths were of course very functional, but they were also very sociable places, where people went to meet and mingle. So this building would have been a focal point of Toledo Roman society, but strictly segregated as the men and women had separate baths.

The water was pulled from the aqueduct, heated in a furnace, and then channeled into the bathing rooms. The rooms were all named depending on how hot the water was, so there was the hot bath, the warm bath, and the cold bath. Toledo society discussed and ran the city while relaxing in this building.

Leave the baths and return to Plaza Amador de los Ríos. The Tolmo Museum stands on the square with shady trees in front of it. Face the museum and walk down its left hand side along Calle Navarro Ledesma. This will take you into another little square called Plaza Tendillas. Turn right into Calle Cardenal Lorenzana and you will see the Lorenzana Palace on your left.

Lorenzana Palace

Cardinal Lorenzana bought up the old building which once stood here - it had been the headquarters of the dreaded Inquisition. He had it flattened and replaced with this beautiful building to be used by the University. You can see how impressive the building is with its double stairway leading up to a grand facade of columns. It's still used by the university, but it's clearly far too grand for the students as it's used for administration now.

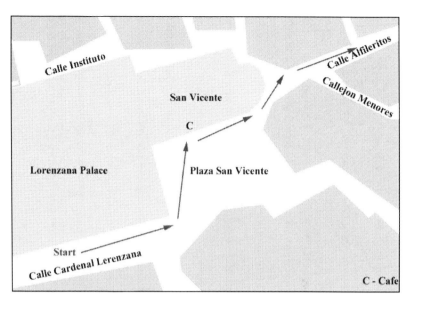

Continue along the front of the Palace and into Plaza San Vicente

San Vicente

On the left-hand side of the square is the church of San Vicente. This poor church has suffered a lot over the centuries, with many alterations and additions. It was deconsecrated in 1842 and after many incarnations is now the headquarters of the Academy of Arts in Toledo. Look at the window directly below the tower - you can see some Visigoth stonework running along the bottom of the window.

If you need refreshment, there is a café inside the Academy of Arts where you can sip your drink inside the old church building.

Exit the church and turn left to walk along the side of the church. Continue straight ahead down Calle Alfileritos, but do turn around to get a good view of the handsome church apse – it's worth a snap.

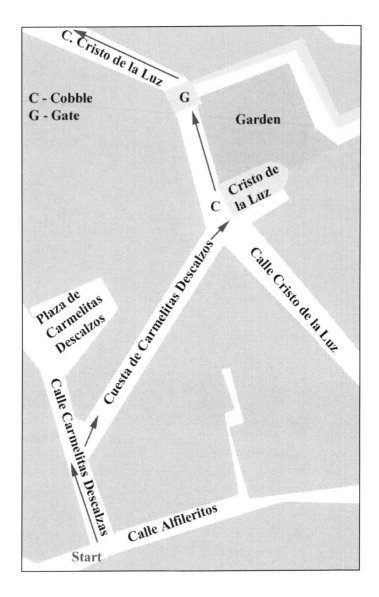

Take the first left, narrow Calle Carmelitas Descalzas, and then the first right, Cuesta de Carmelitas Descalzos.   This will bring you to Cristo de la Luz.

Cristo de la Luz (Tourist Bracelet)

This is a very old building. It was originally a Mosque built on top of a Visigothic church in 999 AD. As you approach the railings, find the single white cobblestone in front of the gate. Of course there is a legend – in fact there are several but this is my favourite.

When King Alfonso took control of Toledo from the Moors, he and his army leaders stopped in this street to see the mosque. When they tried to proceed, the King found his horse would not continue; it then knelt and the King's companions found their horses doing the same. They took it to be a sign that they should go into the Mosque and explore.

They noticed a shaft of light between two stones and ordered the stones to be removed. Inside the wall they found a crucifix and a lamp which had been alight for four centuries, hidden there when the Moors first arrived and took over the Visigoth Christian kingdom. King Alfonso left his shield there with the inscription,

> This is the shield which the King Alfonso VI
> left in this chapel when he conquered Toledo,
> and the first mass was held here

If you have visited Madrid, that story about the crucifix being hidden in a wall might sound very familiar! The white cobblestone was placed in front of the building to mark the moment. The Mosque was then given to the Templar Knights and named Cristo de la Luz to commemorate the miracle.

Inside is small but impressive. The church also has a nice little garden and a good view from the terrace at the back. From there you can clearly see the two halves of the building, the square half of the building is the original mosque and the round apse is the Christian addition.

Exit the church and with the door behind you turn right to go through Puerto Valmardon - It's obviously very old and is probably the oldest gate in the city.

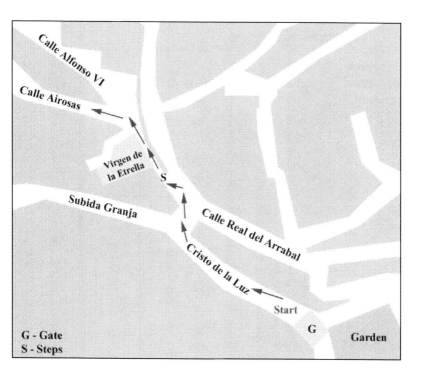

Follow Calle Cristo de la Luz downhill until you reach a junction on your right which gives you access onto Calle Real del Arrabal. Once on Calle Real del Arrabal turn left. Just a few yards further downhill you will reach a little flight of steps leading down to another church, Ermita de la Virgen de la Estrella – The Virgin of the Stars. Before you go down the steps, have a look above the door to see Mary with stars above and below her. Go down the steps now to reach the church door.

Ermita de la Virgen de la Estrella

The original church was built in the fourteenth century by the Brothers of the Garden, and it included a hostel where the poor could take shelter at night. It was demolished and replaced with this church in the seventeenth century.

There is a procession on the last Sunday of May which starts at this church. The people celebrate La Caballada, the charge of Muleteers in 1162 who saved the popular boy King Alfonso from his uncle Ferdinand who wanted to seize the throne. The soldiers in question were travelling by mule on a pilgrimage to honour the Virgin de la Estrella at the time, but raced off to rescue their King when they heard the disturbing news.

There is a mass, with free lemonade and tostones (fried plantain slices). The fun continues with the procession and fireworks. If the church is open, pop in to see the statue of the Virgin Mary which is carried on the procession.

When you exit the church turn left. Ignore the first street which runs along the side of the church. A little further on you will see another two streets leading away from the triangular square - take the first one, Calle Airosas.

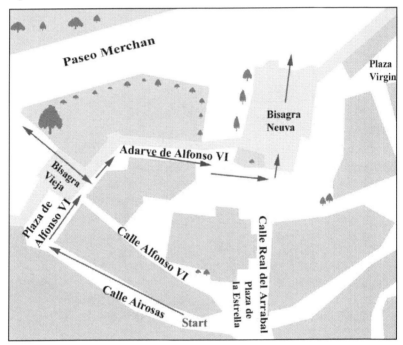

Calle Airosas will take you to Plaza Alfonso VI where you will find the Puerto Alfonso, which used to be called Puerta Bisagra Vieja – The Old Gate.

The Puerta Bisagra Vieja

The old gate was the main entrance to the city, and was built by the Moors in 10th century. You can see the typical horseshoe archway so loved by Moorish architects. The gate's other name is Puerta Alfonso VI because it was through this gate that King Alfonso VI rode into town in 1085 after defeating the Moors.

Pop out to see the city walls and then return inside. Turn left to climb Travesía Adarve de Alfonso VI. This will take you to the best known of the city gates.

Puerta de BiSagra Nueva

This is the most famous of Toledo's gates and it's certainly the most impressive. Inside and high above you will find a rather worn statue of the first Archbishop of Toledo, San

Eugenio. Above him is a plaque which commemorates Good King Wamba:

Erexit fautore Deo Rex inclytus urbem Wamba.

To God and King Wamba the city owes its walls

The other statue inside the gate is Emperor Charles V, son of Joanna the Mad. Walk through and turn around to see that the arch is decorated with a grandiose coat of arms containing a huge two headed eagle – you might guess that it was put up by Emperor Charles V. At the top is an angel with a drawn sword, guarding the city gate.

Now you can take an optional detour. If you have the time and interest you could spend ten minutes walking through the park in front of the gate to reach the Hospital de Tavera. It's a hospital which has become an art gallery and is a place to see some more wonderful El Greco's. There is an entrance fee and be warned, it closes for a long lunch so timing is essential. At the time of writing it closes at 1:30pm until 3:00pm.

You should try to fit a visit in if you have time, but if you would rather skip the hospital continue from "Back into Town".

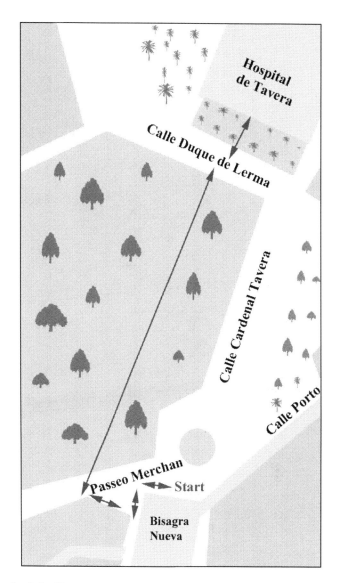

Hospital de Tavera

To visit the hospital you need to walk through the park you can see diagonally left across Paseo Merchan. Make your way carefully across Paseo Merchant to reach it. Walk right through the park – you will probably appreciate the shady trees. At the other end of the park you will reach the Hospital de Tavera fronted with a little hedge garden.

You will pass through a lovely courtyard before first entering the church. The courtyard starred in The Three Musketeers (the version with Oliver Reed in it). It was here that D'Artagnan joined the musketeers to fight the Cardinal's men.

In the church itself you will find the tomb of Cardinal Tavera centre-stage. He was responsible for the construction of the hospital. As you explore, you will probably be able to spot the El Greco paintings by his very distinctive style.

Baptism of Christ – El Greco
El Greco's Baptism of Christ is hanging on the right-hand side of the altar.

The Sacristy is reached by a door on the right of the church, and is where you can find two more El Greco masterpieces.

Sagrada Familia – El Greco

If you visit the Santa Cruz Museum later in this walk, you will see another version of this beautiful painting.

The Tears of Saint Peter – El Greco

The bible tells us that Peter denied knowing Jesus, and "broke down and wept", and here El Greco has painted the remorse Peter later felt.

El Greco painted at least six versions of the sad scene, and you might have already seen a version on Walk 1.

When you exit the museum return through the park to Puerta de Bisagra Nueva and go through the gate once more.

Back into Town

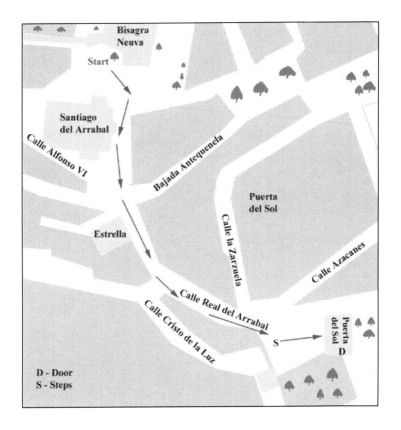

Once through the gate, right in front of you is the Iglesia Santiago del Arrabal.

Iglesia Santiago del Arrabal

I love the translation of this church's name, St James of the Outskirts. The church is one of the most striking Mudejar buildings in Toledo – with typical horseshoe arches and a minaret tower.

If it's open, visit to see the beautiful 14th-century Mudejar pulpit and its ceiling which is said to be one of the most beautiful in Toledo. There are also several interesting tombstones to have a look at.

With the church door behind you, turn right to climb back up Calle Real de Arrabal and pass the Ermita de la Virgen de la Estrella Church you saw earlier. Keep on this street until you can take a few steps up on the right to reach another of Toledo's mighty gates, the Puerta del Sol.

Puerta del Sol

This gate was built by the Templar Knights in the 14th century. Above the archway you can see a white marble block with a sculpture on it. The marble block is a recycled early Christian sarcophagus and the sculpture on it depicts the legend of Saint Ildefonso which you will have already read about. Ildefonso is being given his robe by the Virgin Mary who miraculously appeared during a mass in the Cathedral's Descension Chapel. There is also a sun and a moon at the top of the sculpture but they are rather worn so you need to look carefully. It's the sun which gives the gate its name.

Even higher above the arch you can just make out another small sculpture below a window, and there is a legend about it. During the reign of Ferdinand III, the Governor of Toledo was Fernando Gonzalo. He was hated by the people because he raised taxes as he pleased and forced himself on Toledo's women who were too scared to refuse him. Anyone who dared say no was usually executed.

One day he saw a beautiful woman and expected the same compliance, however he was refused. To force her, the mayor kidnapped her two sons. The young woman fell on her knees in front of King Ferdinand who was in Plaza Zocodover giving a public audience. Once she told her story other people took courage and stood up to tell their tale. The king was outraged and had Gonzalo dragged in front of him and executed. The king ordered this sculpture on the Puerto del Sol to emphasize that the King looks after his people.

Go under the gate. If you are lucky you will find the door on the right open, and if so you can climb up to the top of the gate for good views over Toledo and Castile.

Continue climbing uphill. This will bring you to another gate called the Puerta Alarcones. It was built by the Visigoths and until the Puerto del Sol was built it was the main defensive gate of the city.

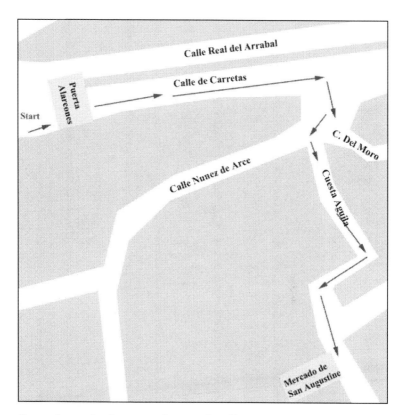

Once through the gate the road will open out and you get a good view of the Castille countryside, including the high dome of the Hospital Tavera.

When you reach the end of the building on your right the road widens. Turn right. You will see a tiny little stepped alley ahead of you - Cuesta Águila. Climb the steps and continue to follow this little alley as it turns right. The alley widens out as it then turns left, and shortly after you will see the Mercado de San Augustine on your right.

Mercado de San Augustine

This old building has been transformed into a very modern marketplace selling only the very best Spanish cuisine, so you could treat yourself. The concept is to promote the best regional and local produce. The goodies are on several floors so you could have a look around to see if you fancy visiting for a meal or drink – the cocktail bar is on the top floor.

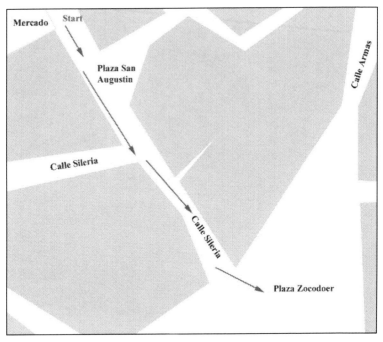

When you leave the market turn right and walk straight ahead across Plaza San Augustine. Continue straight ahead as Calle Sileria merges from the right, and you will soon reach Plaza Zocodover once again.

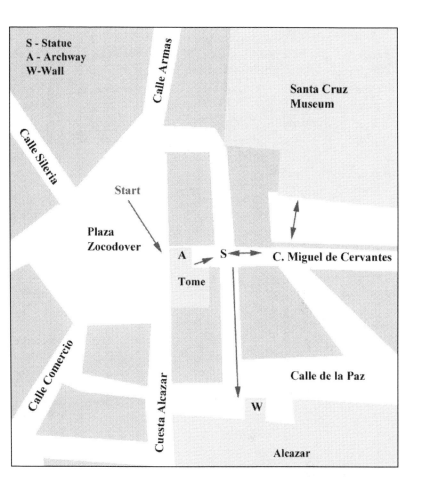

S - Statue
A - Archway
W-Wall

Calle Armas

Santa Cruz Museum

Calle Sileria

Start

Plaza Zocodover

A → S ↔ C. Miguel de Cervantes

Tome

Calle Comercio

Cuesta Alcazar

Calle de la Paz

W

Alcazar

Cross the plaza and go through the Arco de la Sangre archway to leave the square. Descend some steps, and you will find a statue of Cervantes facing downhill.

Cervantes

Cervantes is of course the author of Don Quixote, and probably Spain's most famous author. If you have visited Madrid you will no doubt have toured the literary quarter where he lived and worked.

So why does Toledo have a statue of Cervantes? He wrote a book called "The Illustrious Scullery Maid", which featured two young men who fell in love with the same girl from Toledo. She was said to work in an inn on this street called the Posada de la Sangre. For many years it was thought the inn was the building on the corner of Calle Santa Fe, the next street down from Cervantes – he does seem to be looking at it. However it was later located further down Calle Cervantes, and sadly blown up in the Spanish Civil War.

It's a popular statue, it's reckoned to be photographed as much as Toledo's most famous sights. So if you feel like taking a snap, why not stand next to Cervantes and assume the same pose.

Walk down Calle Cervantes and on your left you will find the Museo de Santa Cruz.

Museo de Santa Cruz

This is Toledo's best museum, full of paintings and artifacts gathered up from Toledo's old religious buildings. It's open from 10:00 am, even on Mondays when most museums are closed.

Have a look at the ornate sculpture above the door, it looks like you are going into a religious building but it was originally a hospital funded by the will of Cardinal Gonzalez. Going into a medieval hospital as a patient was a horrible event – as you were highly likely never to walk out again. But new ideas on hygiene and nursing were just arriving and this hospital was one of the best of its time.

It became a museum in the nineteenth century, and is full of art and ceramics, and would be a must see for fans of El Greco. If you are not interested in visiting skip forward To the Alcazar

The museum is in three sections, Archaeology, fine Arts, and Industrial Arts, and it's most likely you will find the Fine Arts the most interesting. How much you see depends on your time and interest.

The collection is in the large ground floor gallery, and each exhibit is accompanied by information to help the viewer. As you explore don't forget to look up at the gorgeous wooden ceiling.

Here are some highlights to hunt for:

Don Juan's Standard

This enormous flag flew at the helm of Don Juan's flagship, as the fleets of Europe battled with the armada of the invading Turks at Lepanto in the Gulf of Corinth in Greece. It was probably one of the turning points in European history. The Turkish army was already outside Vienna and ready to pour into Europe, and only the crippling defeat at Lepanto stopped them.

Veronica with the Holy Face – El Greco

This painting shows Veronica displaying the miraculous imprint of Christ's face on the cloth used to wipe his brow. You can see why one of the manoeuvres of the Matador with this cape is called a Veronica. It originally hung in Santa Leocadia which you saw on Walk 1.

Sagrada Familia – El Greco

The lady with the very striking face gazing at Jesus is Saint Anne – while Joseph hovers in the background as though not quite sure what to do.

Assumption of the Virgin – El Greco

This very colourful painting is thought to be one of El Greco's masterpieces – he painted it just a year before he died. For anyone who doesn't know, The Assumption is the moment when The Virgin Mary leaves Earth behind, and rises to heaven in a cloud of glory, usually surrounded by angels – an artist's favourite scene. Toledo sits at the bottom of the painting.

Crucifixion – El Greco

This depiction of the crucifixion has Toledo in the background – a trick used by many artists to portray their city as devout and important.

Tapiz de los Astrolabois

If you venture downstairs you will see the museum's tapestry collection which is more interesting than it sounds.

The Astroloabois displays how most people believed the world worked in the 15th century. In the top left corner is God, commanding an angel to turn a crank and make the cosmos move. The cosmos is in the centre filled with signs of the zodiac. On the right are Arithmetic and Geometry portrayed as ladies accompanied by Virgil the astronomer.

Don't miss going into the lovely courtyard and climbing the monumental staircase to the upper floor – even if you only plan to stay a few minutes there.

To the Alcazar

When you have had enough art, exit Santa Cruz museum and turn right to return uphill towards Cervantes. Just before you reach him take the narrow street on the left, Calle de Santa Fe. You will reach Calle de la Paz and the huge building in front of you is part of the Alcazar.

The bit of old wall you see is part of the old Roman wall, and just next to it is the entrance to the Army museum,

Alcazar

The Alcazar sits on the highest part of the city and has been there since the tenth century, although with many alterations over the centuries. Royalty lived there for a while but it then became a Military Academy.

At the start of the Spanish civil war, Toledo sided with the Republicans, but the small and ill-equipped nationalist army installed themselves in the Alcazar, and held it against everything the Republic could throw at them. The fortress was commanded by Commander Moscardo who refused to surrender even to save his son's life. He was phoned by the Republicans and ordered to open the gate or his son would be shot. Moscardo asked to speak to his son, and told him

> "Commend your soul to God and die like a patriot, shouting 'Long live Christ the King' and 'Long live Spain.'"

It's a dramatic story which inspired the defenders. The soldiers repulsed and held the fortress for eight weeks until they were relieved by Franco's army. When the siege ended Moscardo greeted Franco with a salute and said

> "No change to report."

The Siege of the Alcazar was a hugely symbolic victory for Franco's forces, and Franco's press made sure it was reported everywhere in Spain.

If you are interested in armour and weapons you should visit, as it is home to the Military Museum and you will love it – you even get to see Moscardo's office peppered by bullet holes. Don't miss having a good look at the plaques presented to the Alcazar to commemorate the siege; they come from such august bodies as The Chilean Army and the Croatian Nazis.

Otherwise the museum is probably of limited interest to most people and the Alcazar is enjoyed as an iconic building on Toledo's skyline.

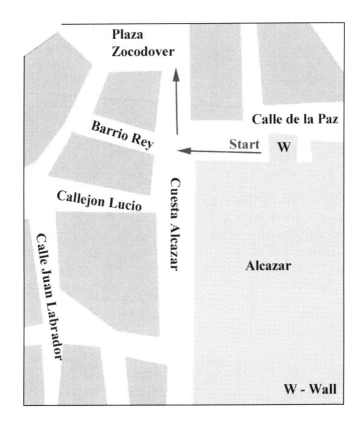

When you are ready to move on, face the Alcazar, and turn right to go along Calle de la Paz to reach Cuesta Alcazar where you turn right to reach Plaza Zocodover where this walk ends.

Did you enjoy these walks?

I do hope you found this walk both fun and interesting, and I would love feedback. If you have any comments, either good or bad, please review this book.

Other Spanish Gems

Why not visit Madrid while you are visiting Spain. It lies just a short a train ride away from Toledo, and is full of interesting sights:

Made in the USA
Middletown, DE
25 February 2020

85322159R00051